LEONARD KUYVENHOV

FORGIVENESS

WHAT THE BIBLE TEACHES
WHAT YOU NEED TO KNOW

LEADER'S GUIDE

FAITH
ALIVE®
Christian Resources

We are grateful to Leonard Kuyvenhoven, pastor of Neland Avenue Christian Reformed Church, Grand Rapids, Michigan, for writing this leader's guide.

We also thank Andrew Kuyvenhoven, Leonard's father, and Leonard for writing the student book for this course. Andrew Kuyvenhoven is a retired pastor in the Christian Reformed Church, author of several books, and former editor of *The Banner.* He lives in Grand Rapids, Michigan.

Unless otherwise indicated, the Scripture quotations in this publication are from the HOLY BIBLE, NEW INTERNATIONAL VERSION, © 1973, 1978, 1984, International Bible Society. Used by permission of Zondervan Bible Publishers.

Faith Alive Christian Resources published by CRC Publications. *Forgiveness: What the Bible Teaches, What You Need to Know. Leader's Guide.* © 2004 by CRC Publications, 2850 Kalamazoo Ave. SE, Grand Rapids, MI 49560.

Any questions or comments about this material? We'd love to hear from you. Call us at 1-800-333-8300 or e-mail us at editors@faithaliveresources.org.

ISBN 1-59255-211-0

10 9 8 7 6 5 4 3 2 1

CONTENTS

LEADING THIS COURSE

Forgiveness: What the Bible Teaches, What You Need to Know explores the biblical teaching of forgiveness as it relates to the forgiveness we receive from God and the forgiveness we are called to extend to one another. These are awesome topics. The forgiveness we receive through the work of Christ is the costliest treasure a Christian possesses. And the task of forgiving others is beyond what any of us is capable of unless God himself is working in us.

It is our hope and prayer that the book and leader's guide may be of some assistance in discovering or discovering anew the liberating news of forgiveness from the pages of Scripture. And it is our conviction that forgiveness is God's answer to our deepest need and his prescription for redeeming the world.

FORMAT

This guide uses a Bible study format. Most of the texts we investigate will be found in the book *Forgiveness*. By studying them together more intensely, participants can discover for themselves some of the depths of the biblical teachings and evaluate the ideas presented in the book.

This guide follows the chapters of the book and outlines materials for seven sessions. We recommend that you take the chapters in sequence.

Each session is designed for approximately sixty minutes. To get the most out of your time together, encourage group members to read the chapter that's up for discussion ahead of time. If most of them do this, it will make your discussion more focused and allow for greater participation and depth in answering the discussion questions.

Make sure everyone gets a copy of the book and understands that they should read the first chapter before coming to the initial group meeting. (The first chapter is brief, so this should not be difficult.) To help you lead this study, this leader's guide has the following features:

- **Chapter Summary.** Each session begins with a brief summary of the chapter from the book to keep the main ideas before you and to refresh your memory. It

may be helpful to highlight some of these key points at the beginning of your time together.

- **Session Goals.** Our goals will be clearly outlined. Generally, there will be two or three primary points in the session. Every session will include questions that ask participants to integrate what has been discussed into their own faith journey.

- **Scripture References.** The passages that the group will use in the session are listed. It will be helpful to have Bibles—in the same version—available for participants. Another possibility is to use a computer program to copy Bible passages and distribute them to participants.

- **Session Handout, Leader's Copy.** Each session includes a leader's copy of the session handout group members will be using. Suggestions for leading the sessions and suggested answers to questions are printed in *type that looks like this*. These answers are intended to be directional, not definitive, pointing you and your group in the direction of a response. They may also be helpful in case you were wondering what the question is supposed to be getting at! You'll also find some optional ideas designed to take the lesson in a different direction, should you wish to do so.

- **Session Handout.** At the end of each session is a handout. Photocopy this and distribute copies to the members of your group at the beginning of each session. This eliminates the need to purchase separate booklets for participants.

As you lead this study, be flexible in the way you use these materials. Take extra time on questions that are of special importance or interest to the group. Feel free to abbreviate others or omit them altogether. The study guide does not treat all matters raised in the book, so you may wish to ask generally what questions the chapter raised for people. Our hope is that the questions will facilitate an open discussion and investigation of the awesome grace and difficult work of forgiveness.

A THEOLOGY OF FORGIVENESS WRAPPED IN A SINGLE STORY

CHAPTER SUMMARY

The first chapter of the book uses the parable of the unmerciful servant to explore the forgiveness God grants and the forgiveness God calls us to extend to one another. The parable is a theology of forgiveness wrapped up in a single story.

Scene 1 is a scene of judgment. A horribly bankrupt debtor appears before his king. The scene depicts our status before God and causes us to investigate the enormity of that debt—the nature of sin. Forgiveness comes as the surprise in the story—beyond what the servant asked for or could have expected. The ground for that forgiveness is not found in anything that the servant does but lies instead in the loving heart of the king.

Scene 2 depicts the just-forgiven debtor coming across a fellow servant who owes him money. The amount pales in comparison to the debt that the king had just forgiven. Despite hearing an impassioned plea for mercy that echoes his own plea for mercy before the king, the unforgiving servant fails to show mercy. The servant refuses to forgive his fellow servant.

In scene 3, judgment day is replayed. This time, judgment is carried out against the unmerciful servant because of his failure to show mercy. The king cannot tolerate this appalling disharmony between mercy received and the failure to extend mercy. This unfitting behavior incurs his wrath and judgment.

The parable teaches that we cannot view forgiveness as a matter of bookkeeping or as a legal obligation. Our calling to forgive others must be seen in the context of God forgiving us. For forgiven people, forgiveness is the only fitting response.

SESSION GOALS

- Walk through the parable of the unforgiving servant, understanding ourselves as part of the story Jesus tells.

- Begin exploring the relationship between having been forgiven and extending forgiveness to others.

- Be challenged to forgive others in the context of God having forgiven us.

SCRIPTURE REFERENCES

Matthew 18:21-35

LEADER'S COPY, HANDOUT: SESSION 1
A THEOLOGY OF FORGIVENESS
WRAPPED IN A SINGLE STORY

Be sure you have made sufficient copies of the handout so that there is one for each participant. You might also take a moment now to explain the format of this study—the handout takes Scripture references from the book and provides discussion questions that will help the group understand and apply the main ideas from each chapter.

INTRODUCTION

The Bible presents forgiveness as our greatest need. Without forgiveness, life together with God would be impossible. And without forgiveness, significant and sustained relationships with other people would be virtually unattainable. In your own experience, what has driven home the importance of forgiveness?

After reading the above, invite participants to share their responses with the group. As leader, break the ice (and give participants time to think) by first giving your own example. After discussion, have someone read aloud the remainder of the introduction.

During the course of this Bible study we will be looking at what the Bible teaches about the forgiveness that God gives us, the forgiveness we are commanded to extend to each other, and the relationship between the two. When asked about forgiveness, Jesus responds by telling the parable that is the central topic of chapter 1. To get a handle on the question "How many times shall I forgive my brother?" we are supposed to understand ourselves as part of the story that Jesus tells.

Option: Alternate Opening

Here's an alternate way to open your session. Begin by asking participants to list—in order of priority—the top three areas of their lives or relationships where forgiveness plays the biggest role (in my relationship with God, with my spouse, with my kids, with fellow employees, at church, and so on). Have people read at least the number one item on their list and see if there's agreement among the group. Then read through the introduction on the handout.

SCENE 1 (VV. 21-27)

Remember, answers given to the questions below are only suggestions meant to point your group in the direction of an answer. They may also be helpful if you were wondering what the question is supposed to be getting at! Be sure to invite the group to ask their own questions too or to comment on statements found in the book.

1. **Why do you think Peter asked his question about forgiveness?**

   Peter's question is a natural extension of Jesus' teaching in the previous verses, where Jesus had been talking about what to do when someone sins against you. Now the down-to-earth man who used to fish for a living simply wants to know exactly how much forgiveness he's obligated to extend to someone. He wants to put some parameters in place. Of course, we can also wonder if perhaps Peter had someone in mind who had recently offended him—but that's sheer speculation, of course.

2. **Put yourself in the position of the servant as he is brought before the king.**

   - **Why is it important to the story that the one to whom the debt is owed is a king?**

     This is not simply an ordinary debtor/creditor relationship. A subject is dependent on the king and owes everything to him. Furthermore, the king has absolute power over the subject. Also, the king image will suggest God and judgment day to those who hear the parable (see p. 9 of the book).

   - **How could the servant have gotten this far into debt?**

     Only by a total disregard for the king's interests.

   - **As he comes before the king, what might he be feeling and thinking about the king? About himself? About his future?**

     Imagine having your freedom taken away and then being told that your wife and children would be sold into slavery to repay your debt! This is a terrible, desperate situation. No doubt he is fervently hoping that the king is a merciful man. Perhaps he is afraid of what the king might say and do. Almost certainly he regrets his deep plunge into debt. He can see only a bleak future for himself and for his family.

   - **The servant pleads for more time so that he can repay the debt himself. How might we do the same thing with God?**

     We might do the same thing when we decide we'll wait to go to God until we have our life neatly cleaned up. We have plans for restoration, but we fail to understand that only God's help can clean up the mess.

3. **Now put yourself in the servant's place as the king "took pity on him, canceled the debt and let him go." What feelings must be going through the servant's mind about himself, about the king, about his future?**

   As as the book says, "The servant came into the scene a captive bound for slavery. He leaves this scene a free man." Imagine his delight, his huge relief, when the king does not merely give him more time to repay his debt but cancels it instead. It is an overwhelming experience! In seconds, he goes from abject hopelessness to complete freedom. We can see him dancing his way out of the palace, blessing the king's graciousness. At least, that's what we'd expect.

SCENE 2 (VV. 28-31)

1. **Why is it significant that the parable describes sins as "debts" that are owed?**

   Our sins are not simply a matter of bad judgment and mistakes. We owe God, in the sense that we have obligations to him.

2. **Our book says it's important not to belittle the debt that the second servant owes the first. Why? Was this a new insight into this parable for you?**

   See the comments in the book under scene 2 (pp. 11-12).

3. How would the impact of the story change if scene 1 were omitted?

Read and discuss the first paragraph in the book under "What We Learn from Scene 2" (p. 12).

4. Why are we so upset by the actions in this scene? What is Jesus teaching us about forgiveness?

Like the servants who were "greatly distressed," we are upset because of the total lack of gratitude and mercy in the forgiven servant—it's unjust, outrageous behavior. "The king's fantastically generous grace has left no impression on the servant," says the book (p. 12). The scene sets our forgiveness of others in the context of God's forgiving us.

SCENE 3 (VV. 32-35)

1. Why is the king so upset with the servant? What does it tell you about the king's reasons (and God's reasons) for forgiving in the first place?

It shows an astonishing lack of gratitude, and it makes one wonder whether the great gift of forgiveness left any impression on the servant or changed him in any way. He acts as if it never happened, as if scene 1 had never occurred. It would follow that God's gracious gift of forgiveness was given to change us, to leave its impression on us. As the book notes, "Forgiving others from a grace-touched heart is a fitting response. In fact, it is the only response" (p. 13).

2. Does the king's treatment of the unforgiving servant strike you as too harsh? Why or why not?

While we may wish for a "second chance" for the servant, his punishment is richly deserved. "Since the servant acted as if the forgiveness did not exist, the king did too" (p. 13).

3. Based on the parable, is God's forgiveness of us limited or unlimited? Conditional or unconditional?

The parable seems to say both. The forgiveness in scene 1 is certainly unlimited and unconditional. Yet by scene 3 we are left asking whether there are strings attached. In other words, God's grace does require a fitting response.

4. What's your reaction to Jesus' warning in verse 35?

You may want to discuss the book's comment that "the parable should not be used to make rigid statements about God (for example, God is bound to forgive only those who forgive). . . . But neither should we feel free to take the edge off of Jesus' story" (pp. 13-14).

CLOSING

"God's forgiving grace may be unmerited, but it must not go unnoticed. The divine forgiveness must leave its impression on us; we are to be shaped by it" (p. 13).

Reflect on this quotation together by discussing what sort of impression it ought to leave on us. Where in our own relationships can we reflect the forgiveness that God has so graciously given us?

For your closing prayer, you may want to first invite people to offer sentence prayers of thanks to God for so graciously forgiving us a debt we can never repay. Then invite participants to silently ask God to help them show the same kind of mercy toward a specific individual or relationship in their lives.

Option: Alternate Closing

Here is a contemplative way to close the session. Ask group members to imagine themselves as the servant in scene 1 of the parable. They may close their eyes, if they wish, as you read the following, pausing after each item to reflect silently.

- *You have been brought into the king's presence because you owe him a huge debt, more than you can ever even begin to repay. What are you feeling and thinking?*

- *The king demands that you repay the debt at once or you will be imprisoned for the rest of your life. What are you feeling and thinking?*

- *You fall on your knees and beg the king to have mercy. You promise to pay every cent of the debt you owe. What are you feeling and thinking?*

- *The king looks at you with compassion and announces that your huge debt is cancelled, forgiven. You do not need to pay him back, ever. You are free! What are you feeling and thinking?*

You may wish to move into a time of praise and thanks to God, inviting group members to pray aloud as they wish.

FOR NEXT TIME

Ask participants to read chapter 2, "Sin and Forgiveness in Biblical History." Encourage them to allow plenty of time for the reading, as it is twice as long as chapter 1.

A THEOLOGY OF FORGIVENESS
WRAPPED UP IN A SINGLE STORY

Introduction

The Bible presents forgiveness as our greatest need. Without forgiveness, life together with God would be impossible. And without forgiveness, significant and sustained relationships with other people would be virtually unattainable. In your own experience, what has driven home the importance of forgiveness?

During the course of this Bible study we will be looking at what the Bible teaches about the forgiveness that God gives us, the forgiveness we are commanded to extend to each other, and the relationship between the two. When asked about forgiveness, Jesus responds by telling the parable that is the central topic of chapter 1. To get a handle on the question "How many times shall I forgive my brother?" we are supposed to understand ourselves as part of the story that Jesus tells.

Scene 1 (vv. 21-27)

1. Why do you think Peter asked his question about forgiveness?

2. Put yourself in the position of the servant as he is brought before the king.

   • Why is it important to the story that the one to whom the debt is owed is a king?

   • How could the servant have gotten this far into debt?

   • As he comes before the king, what might he be feeling and thinking about the king? About himself? About his future?

   • The servant pleads for more time so that he can repay the debt himself. How might we do the same thing with God?

3. Now put yourself in the servant's place as the king "took pity on him, canceled the debt and let him go." What feelings must be going through the servant's mind about himself, about the king, about his future?

Scene 2 (vv. 28-31)

1. Why is it significant that the parable describes sins as "debts" that are owed?

2. Our book says it's important not to belittle the debt that the second servant owes the first. Why? Was this a new insight into this parable for you?

3. How would the impact of the story change if scene 1 were omitted?

4. Why are we so upset by the actions in this scene? What is Jesus teaching us about forgiveness?

Scene 3 (vv. 32-35)

1. Why is the king so upset with the servant? What does it tell you about the king's reasons (and God's reasons) for forgiving in the first place?

2. Does the king's treatment of the unforgiving servant strike you as too harsh? Why or why not?

3. Based on the parable, is God's forgiveness of us limited or unlimited? Conditional or unconditional?

4. What's your reaction to Jesus' warning in verse 35?

Closing

"God's forgiving grace may be unmerited, but it must not go unnoticed. The divine forgiveness must leave its impression on us; we are to be shaped by it" (p. 13).

Reflect on this quotation together by discussing what sort of impression it ought to leave on us. Where in our own relationships can we reflect the forgiveness that God has so graciously given us?

SIN AND FORGIVENESS IN BIBLICAL HISTORY

CHAPTER SUMMARY

Sin is bigger than we are inclined to think, and salvation is greater than any church can tell. Sin is not only that we step over the line but that we miss the goal for which God created us. We just don't have it in us to love God above everything and everybody else. And we are alienated from each other.

The biblical diagnosis for the source of our ills is "sin," a basic distrust of the love and reliability of our Maker. Scripture's prescription for the healing of our condition is a restoration of that trust, or "faith." Getting in touch with forgiveness means first getting in touch with our sin. It takes uncommon wisdom for a person to know that God and God's forgiveness are our greatest needs.

Many of the Old Testament laws and regulations had the purpose of showing God's people that sin and God's holiness do not mix. Through these rules, the great Teacher is saying that much of what we encounter every day is not right, not good, and unacceptable. We must make choices all the time and everywhere. Life with a holy God means a life dedicated to the pursuit of holiness.

The Day of Atonement is the Old Testament's premier example of a God-given means of grace. Note the two main actions of the Day of Atonement: first, a sin-offering as an atonement for sin (a goat); second, the removal of the guilt of the people when the accursed sin-bearer (a second goat) is led away to the wilderness. Most of the words the Bible uses for forgiveness reflect one of these two actions: it's either a covering of the sin of the person or a removal of the guilt of the sinner. The Day of Atonement serves as the Old Testament blueprint of the work of Christ in the New Covenant.

Sometimes we are made to think that sinning is normal for us and forgiving is normal for God. But in the Bible, the wrath of God is his "natural" reaction to sin. Punishment and death are normal, but forgiveness and salvation are miracles. Forgiveness originates in the love of the triune God; it is unique and it is divine.

The New Testament gospel comes with a big surprise. The good news of forgiveness and righteousness (by grace through faith in Jesus Christ) is that judgment has already occurred at the cross of Christ. God's judgment is already in: "There is now [already] no condemnation for those who are in Christ Jesus" (Rom. 8:1).

We are asked to believe that the death of Jesus was the full and final payment for all our sins. When Jesus comes the second time, he does not come to deal with sin but to save those who are eagerly waiting for him. Our sins have been punished. God is righteous and will not punish them twice.

SESSION GOALS

- Explore the connection between the nature of sin and the nature of forgiveness.

- Explain how the Day of Atonement was a blueprint for the work of Jesus.

- Examine some of the biblical pictures of forgiveness.

- Feel assured that in Christ we have already received God's forgiveness and are "freed forever from judgment."

SCRIPTURE REFERENCES

Psalms 32:3-5, 11; 38:4-8; 41:4; 51:1-2, 7; 107:17-20; Isaiah 1:8; 44:21-22; Zechariah 3:1-5; Romans 8:1

LEADER'S COPY, HANDOUT, SESSION 2
SIN AND FORGIVENESS IN BIBLICAL HISTORY

INTRODUCTION

Work with two or three other people in your group to list as many myths as you can about sin and forgiveness. Draw on your reading of chapter 2 but also on your own experience. You have five minutes to complete this activity.

While the study of forgiveness may be appealing, it necessarily also involves studying sin. And that's a topic we may be very reluctant to investigate, especially as it relates to our own lives. "One of the chief reasons humans do not readily embrace the good news of God's forgiveness is that they do not believe they have done anything so wrong that they should seek it," says Hugh D. McDonald in *Forgiveness and Atonement.*

"It takes uncommon wisdom for a person to know that God and God's forgiveness are our greatest needs," says chapter 2 (p. 18). In this session, we'll look at forgiveness and the nature of sin.

Give each group a sheet of newsprint and a marker (or, if this is impractical, distribute paper and pens). Give the groups five minutes to list as many myths about sin and forgiveness as they can. When groups are finished, have them tape their sheet to the wall or otherwise display them. (If groups did use newsprint, have them read off their lists while you record them on your board or on a sheet of newsprint.) Just for fun, see which group has the longest list.

Review the lists together, putting a check by those the group thinks were mentioned or implied in chapter 2. Keep the lists on display as you discuss chapter 2.

Conclude by asking someone to read aloud the rest of the introduction.

Option: Alternate Opening

If you prefer, omit the myth activity and simply ask the group to react to the two quotations in the introduction. Do they agree that sin is not a popular topic these days? If so, why?

FORGIVENESS AND THE NATURE OF SIN

1. We cannot truly appreciate and experience the grace of forgiveness unless we become aware of the nature of our sin. The following definitions of sin are drawn from the first part of chapter 2. Take a few minutes to come up with examples that illustrate sin as

- **stepping over the line (transgressions).**

    Example: We deliberately cross over a line that God has drawn for our good between things that are holy and unholy, edifying or destructive. Perhaps we choose to watch pornographic material or indulge in road rage. In addition, we may even step over the line between Creator and creature—the line Adam and Eve crossed in their desire to "be like God."

- **missing the goal for which God created us.**

    Example: God created us for his pleasure and glory. We are to love God above all else. When we live for ourselves and our own interests, perhaps by making money our prime objective, we miss the whole purpose of life.

- **a basic distrust of the love and reliability of our Maker.**

    Example: We want to take matters into our own hands rather than surrender control of our lives to God. We somehow doubt that God has our best interests in mind. We insist that we know better. So we reserve certain areas of our lives—say our finances or business dealings or entertainment choices—for ourselves. Another possibility—we blame God for the troubles we experience.

- **breaking the tie with God.**

    Example: Like Adam and Eve in the garden after they sinned, we no longer have a close, loving relationship with God. Our sins of pride and distrust keep us distant from God. Perhaps we no longer bother to pray regularly, or we no longer meet with God's people, or we simply live our lives without much awareness of God's presence.

- **alienation from others.**

    Example: "We despise, envy, hate, and murder each other," says chapter 2.

2. Often when people speak of sin they use it as a synonym for "mistake." In other words, our motives are assumed to be good, but we fall because of ignorance or temporary weakness. If this is our view of sin, what is necessary to keep sin in check?

How does it compare with the biblical definitions given above?

If you wish, ask the group to give some current examples of well-meaning people who view their sin as a "mistake" or lapse of judgment. Some public figures are especially adept at this. They sleep with someone else's wife and call it a dumb thing to do. Or they gamble on their own game, reluctantly admit it decades later, then want everyone to forget about it and vote them into the Hall of Fame.

If we think of sin merely as a "mistake," then a better education or a good self-improvement course could keep it in check. The biblical notion of sin is much broader and more comprehensive. Sin is a failure to achieve our destiny. It is "the big obstacle that blocks fellowship with God and hinders peaceful relationships with people" (p. 18).

3. Given the biblical definitions of sin given above, what is the cure for the condition

- of stepping over the line?

    Walking according to the will of God.

- of missing the goal for which we were created?

    Living into our identity as children of God.

- of not trusting the love and reliability of our Maker?

    Faith.

- of breaking ties with God?

    Communion with God.

- of being alienated from others?

    Fellowship.

4. How do the following things deepen our understanding of sin?

- **The law of God**

    Through the law we find out what God desires and realize how far we've fallen short.

- **The Day of Atonement and its context**

    Since this is a major theme of chapter 2, be sure participants are clear on its significance. Please see paragraphs four and five of the "chapter summary" section on this handout. In addition, you may want to talk about how the holiness of God is the context for the Day of Atonement. You could also discuss this statement from the book: "One of the reasons you and I have so much trouble understanding these acts of God [executing Nadab, Abhihu, Uzzah] is that we don't fully comprehend the holiness of God and the sinfulness of people" (p. 21).

    Be open to discuss any questions group members have about this section as well.

- **Our conscience**

    Our conscience can tell us what is not right in us, although our conscience is not infallible. It can be contaminated or calloused.

- **An encounter with someone/something holy**

    Sometimes a shining example of something good points out to us what is rather dim in us. Almost universally in Scripture an encounter with God leaves a person with an intimate knowledge of his or her own sinfulness.

- **The cross of Christ**

    Here is the ultimate teacher of the weight and enormity of sin. It cost God this much to set things back on course.

- **Many years of experience as a Christian**

    Experience is a teacher of sin. We come to know our own weakness and shortcomings and our need for God after years of walking with him in humility. Just ask the older folks in your group!

BIBLICAL PICTURES OF FORGIVENESS

Chapter 2 uses the Day of Atonement to describe two biblical images for forgiveness: the covering of sin and its removal. Scripture offers many other pictures to help us experience the grace and fullness of the truth that God forgives. As you read through these Scriptural images, ask:

- What does each picture tell you about the nature of sin?

- What does it tell you about the nature of forgiveness?

    To save time, you may want to divide the five passages up among individuals or small groups.

1. Psalm 38:4-8; 32:3-5, 11

    *My guilt has overwhelmed me
    like a burden too heavy to bear.
    My wounds fester and are loathsome
    because of my sinful folly.
    I am bowed down and brought very low;
    all day long I go about mourning.
    My back is filled with searing pain;
    there is no health in my body.
    I am feeble and utterly crushed;
    I groan in anguish of heart.*

    —Psalm 38:4-8

When I kept silent,
my bones wasted away
through my groaning all day long.
For day and night
your hand was heavy upon me;
my strength was sapped
as in the heat of summer.
Then I acknowledged my sin to you
and did not cover up my iniquity.
I said, "I will confess
my transgressions to the LORD"—
and you forgave
the guilt of my sin. . . .
Rejoice in the LORD and be glad, you righteous;
sing, all you who are upright in heart!

—Psalm 32:3-5, 11

These texts describe sin as a burden, a crushing weight that bows the sinner to the ground and fills him or her with pain and anguish. Forgiveness is then the lifting of that weight from the sinner, causing him or her to rejoice and be glad and sing.

2. Zechariah 3:1-5

Then he showed me Joshua the high priest standing before the angel of the LORD, and Satan standing at his right side to accuse him. The LORD said to Satan, "The LORD rebuke you, Satan! The LORD, who has chosen Jerusalem, rebuke you! Is not this man a burning stick snatched from the fire?"

Now Joshua was dressed in filthy clothes as he stood before the angel. The angel said to those who were standing before him, "Take off his filthy clothes."

Then he said to Joshua, "See, I have taken away your sin, and I will put rich garments on you." Then I said, "Put a clean turban on his head." So they put a clean turban on his head and clothed him, while the angel of the LORD stood by.

—Zechariah 3:1-5

Sin is portrayed as being dressed in filthy clothes, unfit to be seen in the presence of the shining righteousness of the angel of the Lord. Forgiveness is shown as removing the filthy clothes and replacing them with the "rich garments" of the righteous.

3. Psalm 51:1-2, 7; Isaiah 1:18

Have mercy on me, O God,
according to your unfailing love;
according to your great compassion
blot out my transgressions.
Wash away all my iniquity
and cleanse me from my sin. . . .
Cleanse me with hyssop, and I will be clean;
wash me, and I will be whiter than snow.

—Psalm 51:1-2, 7

"Come now, let us reason together,"
says the LORD.
"Though your sins are like scarlet,
they shall be as white as snow;
though they are red as crimson,
they shall be like wool."

—Isaiah 1:18

Sin is portrayed as dirt or a stain that's difficult to remove. Forgiveness consists of washing and cleansing, resulting in the removal of the dirt or stain.

4. Isaiah 44:21-22

"Remember these things, O Jacob,
for you are my servant, O Israel.
I have made you, you are my servant;
O Israel, I will not forget you.
I have swept away your offenses like a cloud,
your sins like the morning mist.
Return to me,
for I have redeemed you."

—Isaiah 44:21-22

The people, so to speak, are sitting under a mist or a cloud—it makes them wonder whether God sees them and cares for them. Sin has put up this barrier. But the image of forgiveness speaks of the cloud and the mist being swept away, "burned off" so that God's sunlight makes it to the people. God does not forget them. The light will shine, and the sin that separated them will be swept away like the mist that is gone later in the day.

5. Psalm 41:4; 107:17-20

I said, "O LORD, have mercy on me;
heal me, for I have sinned against you."

—Psalm 41:4

Some became fools through their rebellious ways
and suffered affliction because of their iniquities.
They loathed all food
and drew near the gates of death.
Then they cried to the LORD in their trouble,
and he saved them from their distress.
He sent forth his word and healed them;
he rescued them from the grave.

—Psalm 107:17-20

Sin is an illness that leads to death. Forgiveness is healing from God.

Closing

Which of these pictures speaks most powerfully to you of God's forgiveness? Why?

What does it mean in your personal experience to say, "I am forgiven"?

For personal questions like these, be sure to give people time to collect their thoughts. Learn to be comfortable with brief times of silence. And keep participation on a volunteer level, rather than going around the circle and asking everyone to respond.

If no one mentions it, you must say something about the "big surprise" of the gospel (see pp. 30-31)—we are already forgiven people and therefore the judgment on our sins has been punished and our weakness has been overcome. This is powerful comfort for all of us, especially those among us who still fear rejection at the final judgment. This is the "blessed assurance" that God grants to his children. There is no better news than this!

A fine way to end your session is to read Romans 8:1 aloud. Perhaps you can also say Q&A 56 together (see ch. 2, p. 30).

Option: Alternative Approach to the Session

Here's a procedure that you may want to try for this or one of the other sessions, just for variety. It allows you some freedom from following the session guide and gets you a bit more into the book.

Step 1: *Distribute the session guides, and ask someone to read the chapter summary to the group. Place the guides aside.*

Step 2: *Give everyone five minutes (or more if needed) to locate a quote or section from chapter 2, something that caught their attention or surprised them or gave them a new insight or irritated them, or maybe just something they would like to discuss further with the group. Have them mark the location of the quote with a Post-it note. If a Bible passage is associated with the quote, ask them to note the location of that passage as well.*

Step 3: *Use the quotes to structure your discussion. You can do this more systematically by walking through chapter 2 section by section, asking if anyone choose a quote from that section. Ask people to read their quote along with their reasons for choosing it. Don't feel you have to talk at length about every quote. Some may simply be read and appreciated.*

Should you need to prime the pump a bit, here are a few examples of possible quotes for discussion:

- *"It takes uncommon wisdom to know that God and God's forgiveness are our greatest needs" (p. 18).*

- *"One of the reasons you and I have so much trouble understanding these acts of God is that we don't fully comprehend the holiness of God and the sinfulness of people" (p. 21).*

- *"In the Bible, God's forgiveness is not a matter of course. Punishment and death are normal, but forgiveness and salvation are miracles" (p. 24).*

- *The reason why God has mercy on us sinners when we come to him is simply because he is God! He is so different from us that he will forgive! (p. 28).*

- *"The judgment that people fear has already taken place" (p. 30).*

Step 4: *Close by talking about what it means in our personal experience to say, "I am forgiven." You may also want to read Romans 8:1 and Q&A 56.*

SIN AND FORGIVENESS IN BIBLICAL HISTORY

Introduction

Work with two or three other people in your group to list as many myths as you can about sin and forgiveness. Draw on your reading of chapter 2 but also on your own experience. You have five minutes to complete this activity.

While the study of forgiveness may be appealing, it necessarily also involves studying sin. And that's a topic we may be very reluctant to investigate, especially as it relates to our own lives. "One of the chief reasons humans do not readily embrace the good news of God's forgiveness is that they do not believe they have done anything so wrong that they should seek it," says Hugh D. McDonald in *Forgiveness and Atonement.*

"It takes uncommon wisdom for a person to know that God and his forgiveness are our greatest needs," says chapter 2 (p. 18). In this session we'll look at forgiveness and the nature of sin.

Forgiveness and the Nature of Sin

1. We cannot truly appreciate and experience the grace of forgiveness unless we become aware of the nature of our sin. The following definitions of sin are drawn from the first part of chapter 2. Take a few minutes to come up with examples that illustrate sin as

   • stepping over the line (transgressions).

   • missing the goal for which God created us.

   • a basic distrust of the love and reliability of our Maker.

   • breaking the tie with God.

   • alienation from others.

2. Often when people speak of sin they use it as a synonym for "mistake." In other words, our motives are assumed to be good, but we fall because of ignorance or temporary weakness. If this is our view of sin, what is necessary to keep sin in check?

   How does it compare with the Biblical definitions given above?

3. Given the Biblical definitions of sin given above, what is the cure for the condition

   • of stepping over the line?

   • of missing the goal for which we were created?

   • of not trusting the love and reliability of our Maker?

   • of breaking ties with God?

- of being alienated from others?

1. Psalm 38:4-8; 32:3-5, 11

4. How do the following things deepen our understanding of sin?

2. Zechariah 3:1-5

- The law of God

3. Psalm 51:1-2, 7; Isaiah 1:18

- The Day of Atonement and its context

4. Isaiah 44:21-22

- Our conscience

5. Psalm 41:4; 107:17-20

- An encounter with someone/something holy

Closing

Which of these pictures speaks most powerfully to you of God's forgiveness? Why?

- The cross of Christ

- Many years of experience as a Christian

What does it mean in your personal experience to say, "I am forgiven"?

Biblical Pictures of Forgiveness

Chapter 2 uses the Day of Atonement to describe two biblical images for forgiveness: the covering of sin and its removal. Scripture offers many other pictures to help us experience the grace and fullness of the truth that God forgives. As you read through these Scriptural images, ask:

- What does each picture tell you about the nature of sin?

- What does it tell you about the nature of forgiveness?

JESUS AND THE FORGIVENESS OF SIN

CHAPTER SUMMARY

The New Testament opens with the liberating announcement that the wait is over! To those who are burdened by sin but have placed their hope in the unfailing love of God, the angel announces that the time of deliverance has come. God has come to deliver his people from sin. Jesus' name is itself a testimony to the fact that his mission is to save his people from their sin.

The chapter surveys the gospel stories where Jesus grants forgiveness either explicitly or implicitly. In these accounts, forgiveness generally comes as a surprise—beyond what was expected or even requested. The key in the stories is not the behavior of those forgiven, but the heart of the One doing the forgiving. He grants forgiveness as a gift. He goes looking to grant forgiveness to the sinful as much as or more than any of them are seeking to be forgiven. Those who came to him did not need a detailed knowledge about him or completely pure motives. Our faltering steps toward him, our baby steps of faith, are lavishly rewarded with a gift of forgiveness beyond our asking and beyond our comprehension.

The gospels portray the forgiveness we receive through Christ's death by means of symbols. Chapter 3 explores the symbol of the Lord's Supper, especially as it fulfills the Old Testament Passover. In the Lord's Supper, we celebrate the victory God gives us over sin. The victory is accomplished through the poured-out blood of Christ. He is our Passover lamb. Partaking of the supper impresses on us the deliverance that is ours and strengthens us to live in that assurance.

The other symbol explored in this chapter is the rending of the temple curtain at the time of Jesus' death. The torn curtain says in symbolic language what the death of Christ means: the sacrifice is complete and God has accepted it. We have been forgiven and we have been cleansed. Now God's people may approach him boldly.

SESSION GOALS

- Examine forgiveness as the central focus of Jesus' ministry.

- Explore the relationship between faith and forgiveness.

- Deepen our appreciation for the Lord's Supper as a God-given means to strengthen our faith in the forgiveness he has won for us.

SCRIPTURE REFERENCES

Luke 7:36-50; 15:11-32; Psalm 118:27-29

LEADER'S COPY, HANDOUT, SESSION 3
JESUS AND THE FORGIVENESS OF SIN

INTRODUCTION

What images (pictures) come to mind when you think of God as a forgiving God? How have these images helped you in your spiritual walk?

In today's session, we'll examine forgiveness as the central focus of Jesus' ministry, explore the relationship between faith and forgiveness, and deepen our appreciation for the Lord's Supper as a God-given means to strengthen our faith in the forgiveness he has won for us.

If group members have difficulty with this question, rephrase it along these lines: "When God forgives me, I see him as . . ." If you like, you could suggest some examples: a father running to embrace a wandering child who has returned home; wiping a slate clean; removing a stain; cleansing; exchanging dirty clothing for new clothing; removal of our sins from us as far as east is from west. Images such as these can make forgiveness more concrete and real to us. They can help us know for sure that our sins are forgiven and remind us of the deep and amazing love of God.

If you're leading a large group, you could have participants gather in small groups of two to four persons each to discuss this question.

Invite each group member to recall (privately) a recent time when he or she experienced God's forgiveness of some offense, large or small. Allow a minute or so of reflection, then lead group members in a prayer of thanks to God for his forgiveness.

JESUS ANOINTED BY A SINFUL WOMAN
(LUKE 7:36-50)

Ask someone to read this story aloud as the others follow along in their Bibles.

Today's session has a lot of wonderful content to discuss. The parable of the forgiving father is by itself rich enough to last the entire session and beyond! If the group gets involved with one topic, don't hesitate to drop others. There's no need to cover everything.

1. **What do you think prompted the woman to come to the party?**

   In verse 47 Jesus says that her motivation was love. She simply wanted to show Jesus her love and adoration. That's why she did what she did. However, the NIV Study Bible notes (v. 37) suggest that she may have heard Jesus preach and came "in repentance, determined to lead a new life. She came out of love and gratitude, in the understanding that she could be forgiven." Perhaps. Or maybe being forgiven by Jesus was a grace-filled surprise for her.

2. **What words would you use to describe her actions?**

   The woman was courageous. She went to a party where she was clearly out of place and unwanted; once there, she boldly approached Jesus and performed an act of public adoration, finally breaking yet another social convention by wiping Jesus' feet with her hair. She was trusting. She had to have faith that Jesus would not only listen to her but also forgive her (see v. 50). She was unselfish and loving and lavish, sparing no financial or personal expense to show her feelings toward Jesus.

3. **How do Jesus' parable and his words to Simon explain the woman's actions?**

   In stark contrast to Simon, the woman has received Jesus with all the hospitality at her disposal. Jesus' granting forgiveness is connected to the welcoming, loving actions of the woman. "Her many sins are forgiven—for she loved much," says Jesus. By contrast, Simon "loved little" because he had been "forgiven little." Yet it is not the woman's loving actions that saved her but her faith (v. 50).

4. **Perfume was a precious commodity in Jesus' day. Another passage mentions that a bottle cost a year's wages. If you had a year's wages to show Christ your love, what would you do?**

   Perhaps the question will lead to a discussion of how we can be more lavish and unselfish in showing our love for Christ.

5. **Based on this story, what would you say it takes to be forgiven by Jesus?**

   You may want to refer to the comments in chapter 3 about people being drawn to Jesus because "they are looking for something and they see him as the answer. . . . Sometimes Jesus calls it faith" (p. 42).

THE PARABLE OF THE FORGIVING FATHER
(LUKE 15:11-32)

Ask someone to read this story aloud as the others follow along in their Bibles.

1. **Some Bible teachers say that one key to interpreting parables is to look out for the "surprises." What surprises are there in this parable?**

   The son asking for his inheritance is an unpleasant surprise. The father graciously granting that request is another. The son's deciding to return home may also be a surprise. But the biggest surprise of all is the loving embrace of the father, who runs down the road to greet his wayward son and welcomes him home with unconditional, forgiving love.

2. **The prodigal's request for his share of the inheritance is an outrageous demand. What does it say about the father that he grants such a request? What does it tell us about God? About us?**

   It speaks of God's respect for our free will. He allows people to basically say to him, "Father, give me my inheritance; let's pretend you are dead."

3. What brings the prodigal son "to his senses"?

Hunger and the realization that the hired hands on his dad's farm are better off than he is.

4. What does the prodigal's prepared speech (vv. 18-19) tell us about how he viewed what he had done? Do you find his repentance sincere? Appropriate? Deep enough?

Chapter 3 argues that his plan to make things right seems to focus just on restitution of the money—there is no mention of the Father's broken heart and ruined reputation. Yet his request for forgiveness—"I have sinned against heaven and against you"—may be sincere if we regard "coming to his senses" as a kind of spiritual awakening. But since the parable's focus is on the love of the forgiving father, its impact is only increased if the son's homecoming was motivated by something other than genuine repentance.

5. What part does the son's prepared speech play in getting back into the family?

None. The father's embrace interrupts the speech. The son's restoration is by nothing less than the pure grace of the father.

6. What motivates the father to let the son back into the family?

Love for his son and joy that the lost one has returned. He seems to see it all in a resurrection sort of light: "The one who was dead is alive again!"

Option: Contemplating the Story

In Space for God, Don Postema suggests imagining ourselves into this parable. The exercise is meant to have us "experience" the text as though it were happening to us and then to reflect on the text out of our own experience.

To do this with your group (probably after discussing the questions above), ask them to close their eyes and imagine themselves as the son or daughter who is leaving home. Read these statements, pausing after each to allow time for participants to reflect silently for a few seconds:

- *See yourself saying goodbye to your father and family. What are you feeling? Why are you leaving home?*

- *See yourself in the far country. What is it like to be away?*

- *See yourself alone, without friends, money gone. What are you feeling now?*

- *See yourself deciding to return home. What changed your mind?*

- *See your father running down the road toward you, as if he had been watching and waiting for you to return. Are you surprised? What are you thinking and feeling?*

- *See yourself being embraced by the father, your carefully rehearsed speech not needed, his forgiveness and love so obvious. Hear the father say, "This child of mine was dead and has come back to life. This child of mine was lost and is found."*

- *See yourself feasting and rejoicing at the banquet the father has given in your honor.*

Postema suggests concluding by repeating (silently) to oneself: "I belong to God." Allow a minute or so for this.

THE LORD'S SUPPER

1. Does understanding the Lord's Supper in the light of the Old Testament Passover celebration deepen its meaning for you? If so, how?

You may want to re-read some of chapter 3 to set the stage for talking about this question. Here's one possible excerpt: "The Passover was given by God as a means for God's people to focus their trust on his deliverance. To celebrate the feast was to re-ignite hope. And it encouraged the people to open themselves up to praise God. . . . To 'remember' in this way gave the people confidence to face difficulties in the present and gave them hope for the future" (p. 44).

2. Chapter 3 makes the connection between spiritual renewal and the celebration of the Lord's Supper. How does taking the Lord's Supper help you to live out your faith? What part of taking the Lord's Supper is most meaningful to you?

As a lead-in to this discussion, you may want to read the paragraph from chapter 3 that begins: "The Lord's Supper teaches us to look back . . ." (p. 46). Then invite group members to comment on how the supper has been helpful and meaningful to their faith-journeys.

A BURST OF PRAISE

To close, take some time to hear and reflect on the words of Psalm 118:27-29. These would have been the last verses that Christ sang with his disciples after celebrating the Passover before he went out to the garden of Gethsemane to be our Passover lamb. And they are our response of praise to his sacrifice.

Ask someone to read these verses aloud to the group.

JESUS AND THE FORGIVENESS OF SIN

Introduction

What images (pictures) come to mind when you think of God as a forgiving God? How have these images helped you in your spiritual walk?

In today's session, we'll examine forgiveness as the central focus of Jesus' ministry, explore the relationship between faith and forgiveness, and deepen our appreciation for the Lord's Supper as a God-given means to strengthen our faith in the forgiveness he has won for us.

Jesus Anointed by a Sinful Woman (Luke 7:36-50)

Ask someone to read this story aloud as the others follow along in their Bibles.

1. What do you think prompted the woman to come to the party?

2. What words would you use to describe her actions?

3. How do Jesus' parable and his words to Simon explain the woman's actions?

4. Perfume was a precious commodity in Jesus' day. Another passage mentions that a bottle cost a year's wages. If you had a year's wages to show Christ your love, what would you do?

5. Based on this story, what would you say it takes to be forgiven by Jesus?

The Parable of the Forgiving Father (Luke 15:11-32)

Ask someone to read this story aloud as the others follow along in their Bibles.

1. Some Bible teachers say that one key to interpreting parables is to look out for the "surprises." What surprises are there in this parable?

2. The prodigal's request for his share of the inheritance is an outrageous demand. What does it say about the father that he grants such a request? What does it tell us about God? About us?

3. What brings the prodigal son "to his senses"?

4. What does the prodigal's prepared speech (vv. 18-19) tell us about how he viewed what he had done? Do you find his repentance sincere? Appropriate? Deep enough?

5. What part does the son's prepared speech play in getting back into the family?

6. What motivates the father to let the son back into the family?

The Lord's Supper

1. Does understanding the Lord's Supper in the light of the Old Testament Passover celebration deepen its meaning for you? If so, how?

2. The chapter makes the connection between spiritual renewal and the celebration of the Lord's Supper. How does taking the Lord's Supper help you to live out your faith? What part of taking the Lord's Supper is most meaningful to you?

A Burst of Praise

To close, take some time to hear and reflect on the words of Psalm 118:27-29. These would have been the last verses that Christ sang with his disciples after celebrating the Passover before he went out to the garden of Gethsemane to be our Passover lamb. And they are our response of praise to his sacrifice.

THE PROCLAMATION OF FORGIVENESS BY THE CHURCH

CHAPTER SUMMARY

The awesome power of forgiveness resides in the church because Christ is present among his people. The power to forgive sins or to withhold forgiveness belongs to the apostolic teaching as entrusted to the church of Jesus Christ. In other words, the gospel is the power of salvation to everyone who believes! Therefore we must hold to the truth of the gospel, not as if, but because our lives depend on it.

The proclamation of the forgiveness of sins in the name of Jesus is part of the Great Commission. In the book of Acts, the apostles began to fulfill their assignment from Jerusalem and "to the ends of the earth." They required repentance and baptism as the condition for forgiveness and assured the believers of the gift of the Holy Spirit. The faithful church of Christ is still commissioned to extend to its generation a worldwide call for repentance, a proclamation of forgiveness in the name of Jesus, and the beginning of the new world in the gift of the Holy Spirit.

Repentance means a turning from sin to the service of the true God. Repentance results from sorrow for sin. It's the insight that one's life is misdirected. Because of the primacy of God's love and the free nature of God's grace, it is going too far to say that God's forgiveness depends on our repentance. But only repentant sinners are in the right state to accept forgiveness. Repentance and forgiveness are inseparable; you simply cannot have one without the other.

Forgiven sinners cannot remain who they were but must become holy. And that takes pain and effort. Once we are on the right path, we need alertness and prayerful support to stay on the right path. For that reason Christians need daily forgiveness. We receive God's forgiveness when we humbly pray to him, confessing our sins and pleading on his promises.

Today many Protestant denominations have no official form of a confession of sin except in the liturgy of their public worship. This liturgical "service of reconciliation" is repeated every Sunday morning. Actually it is an awesome event if we believe the promise of the Master that he himself is present at that moment. But the routine may dull us to this weekly encounter in which we escape God's deserved punishment and taste his everlasting goodness. Churches and church members must be continually looking for ways to examine their lives in the light of God's will. And the practice of confessing sins and hearing the words of forgiveness must remain healthy and vibrant—because it lies at the heart of the Christian life.

SESSION GOALS

- Examine the church's mission to bring the gospel of forgiveness to the world.

- Explore the relationship between forgiveness and repentance.

- Assess the role of confession and self-examination in our personal lives.

SCRIPTURE REFERENCES

Psalm 130; Matthew 28:18-20; Luke 24:36-49

LEADER'S COPY, HANDOUT, SESSION 4
THE PROCLAMATION OF FORGIVENESS
BY THE CHURCH

INTRODUCTION

"Increasingly today's Christians feel the need for more opportunities to confess sin and to deepen their knowledge of salvation" (p. 62). How true is this for you? Use 10 for "very true to my own experience" and 1 for "not at all true to my own experience." Please don't feel you must agree with the statement! Be candid in assessing your own feelings.

Today's session will focus on the church's role in proclaiming forgiveness, explore the relationship between forgiveness and repentance, and help us assess the role of confession and self-examination in our personal lives.

Take a moment to give group members a chance to report how they rated the statement above. Use a light approach here that encourages an honest reaction—there are no right or wrong answers, of course.

Option: Aternate Opening

If group members are familiar with the Bible, ask them what passages or verses they find particularly comforting as far as forgiveness of our sins is concerned. Give them time to locate a passage, then invite persons to read their passage and tell why it is especially assuring to them.

CARRYING OUT THE GREAT COMMISSION (LUKE 24:36-49)

Ask someone to read Luke 24:36-49 aloud as the others follow along in their Bibles.

1. **Why is it significant that Jesus' final greeting, after his resurrection and immediately prior to his ascension, was "peace be with you"?**

   It is a summary of the gospel. Through Jesus' completed work we have peace—it is ours forever! The disciples will need that peace to be abundantly present as they begin the challenging work Jesus is about to assign them.

2. **By the power of the Holy Spirit and by Jesus guiding them through the Scriptures, the disciples' minds are opened to the plan of God. What part do they (and we) play in that plan? What is our task? How is it a comfort that our part was anticipated already in the Old Testament?**

   The preaching of forgiveness in Jesus' name to all nations is the disciples' task and ours. It's a comfort to know that this was anticipated already in the Old Testament because it confirms that this is God's will. It has been God's plan all along, and God will fulfill his plan through us.

3. **What promise does Jesus make to the disciples as he gives them their task? How is this a comfort?**

   The Holy Spirit will come. It's the "power from on high" spoken about in verse 49. God not only gives the task, but also gives the power to accomplish the task.

4. **Now look at the Great Commission as it is found in Matthew 28:18-20. How does Luke's account help us to understand the Great Commission in Matthew?**

   Forgiveness of sins is the heart of the message, which the disciples take as they go and make disciples.

5. **If someone were to ask you if your church has the power to forgive sins and to withhold forgiveness, what would you say?**

   You will want to refer to the end of the section "A Risky Transfer?" (p. 52) and paragraph one of the chapter summary as you discuss this question. You may also want to look at the sidebar on apostolic succession (p. 53). The heart of the power of the church to forgive or to withhold forgiveness lies in Christ's presence with his church and with the church's presentation of the gospel message. The Heidelberg Catechism puts it this way (Answer 84):

   According to the command of Christ: The kingdom of heaven is opened by proclaiming and publicly declaring to all believers, each and every one, that, as often as they accept the gospel promise in true faith, God, because of what Christ has done, truly forgives all their sins. The kingdom of heaven is closed, however, by proclaiming and publicly declaring to unbelievers and hypocrites that, as long as they do not repent, the anger of God and eternal condemnation rest on them.

REPENTANCE AND FORGIVENESS

"Repentance results from sorrow for sin. It's the insight that one's life is misdirected. This sadness about a wasted life is the beginning of conversion. Repentance, if genuine, is followed by a complete U-turn. There must be a break with the old and a conscious turning toward God. Many Bible teachers stress that both elements are necessary for a complete conversion" (p. 57).

1. **What part does guilt play in true repentance? Is guilt really good for us?**

   True repentance involves seeing yourself as responsible for the misdirection of your life. You don't shrug off your sin ("It couldn't be helped!") or rationalize it away ("Everybody does it!"). You declare yourself guilty. Of course, obsessing about our guilt isn't good for us and isn't what the Lord wants. Such an attitude can make us doubt our salvation and can drive us to despair. Our guilt is not awakened so that we will be condemned. Still, we do need to acknowledge our guilt before the Lord. Those with no sense of guilt deceive them-

selves and see no need for God and forgiveness. Acknowledging our guilt gives us hope for our deliverance.

2. Once guilt is discovered, that's not the end of repentance. For repentance to be complete, it must be accompanied by a turning away from the old and a turning toward God. In your experience, what has making this U-turn been like?

The "about face" of repentance is often difficult and downright unpleasant—and it's something we need to do time and time again. It may involve turning our back on something that exerts an enormous pull on us. It may involve running away from temptation. It may involve asking someone for forgiveness. In his book A Sure Thing, *Cornelius Plantinga quotes C. S. Lewis saying that repentance is a special problem to us because only bad people need to do it and only good people can do it.*

3. How does the process of repentance truly put us in touch with a God who is *both* holy and loving?

In repentance we know that we have fallen short of the demands of God—that puts us in touch with God's holiness. But in repentance we turn toward a God who graciously forgives because of his everlasting love.

4. Why is it "going too far" to say that repentance is the condition for God's forgiveness? How would you explain the connection between forgiveness and repentance?

Note the third paragraph of the chapter summary and "The Relationship Between Repentance and Forgiveness" (pp. 57-58). Does your group agree that "no matter how you put it in theory, in life you cannot have forgiveness without repentance"?

CONFESSION, FORGIVENESS, AND RENEWAL

1. Most Protestant churches have done away with the practice of the confessional. What advantages might there be to confessing your sins to another human in this way? Disadvantages?

*Luther viewed private confession as "the one and only remedy for troubled consciences," and Calvin spoke of the "comfort" of the gospel that pastors can provide those troubled by their sins. Scripture itself encourages us to con-*fess our sins to one another (James 5:16). Disadvantages might include a mistaken sense that the power to forgive sins has been transferred from Christ to the clergy and that our acts of contrition contribute to our forgiveness. In addition, recital of our sins in exchange for forgiveness can become something of a mechanical ritual. No doubt group members will mention other advantages and disadvantages as well.*

2. "Today many Protestant denominations have no official form of confession of sin except in the liturgy of their public worship" (p. 60). This liturgical "service of reconciliation" is repeated every Sunday morning in most of our liturgies. When has the service of reconciliation been most helpful for you? What were the conditions that made it helpful?

You might note the statement from chapter 4 that the "service of reconciliation" can be "an awesome event if we believe the promise of the Master that he himself is present at that moment" (p. 61).

3. Since Christians are already forgiven by the work of Christ, why do we still ask for forgiveness on a daily basis?

It's part of the process of sanctification. Getting our lives in step with the Spirit and in line with the will of God takes continual self-examination and a process of asking God to forgive what is in us that is against his will.

4. Take a moment to reflect on the role of confession and self-examination in your own life. Has anything in chapter 4 or this session offered a possible way to enrich and deepen that role? Do you have other ideas for accomplishing this? Please share your thoughts with the group.

We hope that your study group has become a place where people have come to know and trust each other enough to respond to a question like this. Confession is deeply personal— yet, because it is at the heart of our walk with God, we need to be able to talk about it and practice it with each other.

CLOSING

Read Psalm 130 as the prayer of a repentant sinner who approaches God from "out of the depths," who acknowledges his or her sin, who waits for the Lord, and who finds unfailing love and full redemption.

Option: Study of Psalm 130

If you have time, you may want to discuss Psalm 130 before reading it meditatively as your prayer of confession. Here are a couple of questions to discuss:

- What are "the depths" (v. 1)?

- How does the rest of the psalm help to fill that in for us?

    The writer acknowledges his guilt—he addresses God from "out of the depths" of despair over his sin. The remainder of the psalm focuses on God's mercy and unfailing love, on which the writer waits and on which he pins all his hope and assurance.

- How do you understand verse 4—what is the relationship between God being forgiving and "feared"? Does that help your understanding of what Scripture means by "the fear of the Lord"?

    Forgiveness is such an awesome act of God that we who are forgiven desire to do his will. Fear of the Lord is not some sort of terror, but a deep desire to do God's will, a desire that comes from experiencing God's awesome and forgiving presence.

THE PROCLAMATION OF FORGIVENESS BY THE CHURCH

INTRODUCTION

"Increasingly today's Christians feel the need for more opportunities to confess sin and to deepen their knowledge of salvation" (p. 62).

How true is this for you? Use 10 for "very true to my own experience" and 1 for "not at all true to my own experience." Please don't feel you must agree with the statement! Be candid in assessing your own feelings.

Today's session will focus on the church's role in proclaiming forgiveness, explore the relationship between forgiveness and repentance, and help us assess the role of confession and self-examination in our personal lives.

CARRYING OUT THE GREAT COMMISSION
(LUKE 24:36-49)

1. Why is it significant that Jesus' final greeting, after his resurrection and immediately prior to his ascension, was "peace be with you"?

2. By the power of the Holy Spirit and by Jesus guiding them through the Scriptures, the disciples' minds are opened to the plan of God. What part do they (and we) play in that plan? What is our task? How is it a comfort that our part was anticipated already in the Old Testament?

3. What promise does Jesus make to the disciples as he gives them their task? How is this a comfort?

4. Now look at the Great Commission as it is found in Matthew 28:18-20. How does Luke's account help us to understand the Great Commission in Matthew?

5. If someone were to ask you if your church has the power to forgive sins and to withhold forgiveness, what would you say?

REPENTANCE AND FORGIVENESS

"Repentance results from sorrow for sin. It's the insight that one's life is misdirected. This sadness about a wasted life is the beginning of conversion. Repentance, if genuine, is followed by a complete U-turn. There must be a break with the old and a conscious turning toward God. Many Bible teachers stress that both elements are necessary for a complete conversion" (p. 57).

1. What part does guilt play in true repentance? Is guilt really good for us?

2. Once guilt is discovered, that's not the end of repentance. For repentance to be complete, it must be accompanied by a turning away from the old and a turning toward God. In your experience, what has making this U-turn been like?

3. How does the process of repentance truly put us in touch with a God who is *both* holy and loving?

4. Why is it "going too far" to say that repentance is the condition for God's forgiveness? How would you explain the connection between forgiveness and repentance?

CONFESSION, FORGIVENESS, AND RENEWAL

1. Most Protestant churches have done away with the practice of the confessional. What advantages might there be to confessing your sins to another human in this way? Disadvantages?

2. "Today many Protestant denominations have no official form of a confession of sin except in the liturgy of their public worship" (p. 60). This liturgical "service of reconciliation" is repeated every Sunday morning in most of our liturgies. When has the service of reconciliation been most helpful for you? What were the conditions that made it helpful?

3. Since Christians are already forgiven by the work of Christ, why do we still ask for forgiveness on a daily basis?

4. Take a moment to reflect on the role of confession and self-examination in your own life. Has anything in chapter 4 or this session offered a possible way to enrich and deepen that role? Do you have other ideas for accomplishing this? Please share your thoughts with the group.

CLOSING

Read Psalm 130 as the prayer of a repentant sinner who approaches God from "out of the depths," who acknowledges his or her sin, who waits for the Lord, and who finds unfailing love and full redemption.

THE PRACTICE OF FORGIVENESS IN THE CHURCH: SELF-DISCIPLINE AND MUTUAL DISCIPLINE

CHAPTER SUMMARY

God's forgiveness and our acts of forgiveness are of one and the same substance: grace! The source of grace is God. The followers of Jesus live by this grace, and if we don't have it, we don't belong to his disciples. The church is the place where forgiveness is received, proclaimed, and practiced. Forgiveness and the church are so closely linked that from the earliest creeds of the church, they are found in the same breath. Baptism, which symbolizes that cleansing from our sin, defines who we are as people of Christ, and initiates us into the community of the forgiven.

Forgiveness and salvation are not ultimately dependent on our identifying and confessing our sins. It's not a matter of making sure we "die with a clean slate." We are saved by God's grace through the forgiveness earned by Christ. Nothing else can do it for you or for me. Just trust that your Savior cleans the slate—even to the last stains.

As God's people, the community of forgiven sinners, the church must be committed to keeping out all sin and worldliness. Christ died to defeat these things; we cannot turn around and embrace them. We promote holiness and combat sinfulness on three levels:

- Self-discipline. We may come to Jesus as we are, but we cannot stay the way we were. Now we fight against sin with all our might because we don't want to fall back into the slavery of the old tyrant. We are called to grow in holiness.

- Mutual discipline. We are connected to one another as the different members of our body are, in mutual dependence. The Bible teaches that there is no such thing as an unattached member of the body of Christ, just as your body and mine do not have unattached members and organs. We cannot have a love relationship with God if we refuse a love relationship with God's children. That love is also expressed by admonishing those who sin without being judgmental and with the obvious intention to bring the sinner home. The "manual" for confronting someone stuck in sin is found in Matthew 18.

The third type of discipline—official or church discipline—is discussed in chapter 6.

Note: If your group members are comfortable with a longer reading assignment, you may want to combine chapters 5 and 6 into a single session. We've broken up the chapter on the church and forgiveness simply because of the large amount of material covered.

SESSION GOALS

- Explore the relationship between forgiveness and self-discipline and mutual discipline.

- Evaluate the "dying with a clean slate" view of forgiveness and salvation.

- Look at the method given by Christ to confront those who have sinned against us.

SCRIPTURE REFERENCES

Matthew 18

LEADER'S COPY, HANDOUT, SESSION 5
THE PRACTICE OF FORGIVENESS IN THE CHURCH:
SELF-DISCIPLINE AND MUTUAL DISCIPLINE

INTRODUCTION

Stanza 42 of *Our World Belongs to God: A Contemporary Testimony* nicely summarizes what this session is all about. To open today's session, you may want to read it together.

The church is a gathering of forgiven sinners,
called to be holy,
dedicated to service.
Saved by the patient grace of God,
we deal patiently with others.
Knowing our own weakness and failures,
we bring good news to all sinners
with understanding of their condition,
and with hope in God.

In today's session we'll explore the relationship between forgiveness and discipline, taking a detailed look at Matthew 18 and at self-discipline and mutual discipline.

Option: Alternate Opening

If possible (and not too embarrassing!) share with the group an incident where you needed correcting by a brother or sister in Christ. What difference did it make to you? Did you see it as an act of love? If you wish, invite the group to share their own examples.

FORGIVENESS AND DISCIPLINE

1. How would you respond, or what guidance would you give, to someone in your church or small group Bible study who said:

- "I keep failing to live like I know I should. I feel like a failure as a Christian. I'm sick and tired of going back to God with the same old sins, asking for forgiveness again and again. And I bet God feels the same way."

  This quote shows someone who is committed to living the Christian life but who continues to struggle with a particular sin or sins. The person's guilt and discouragement are obvious. In such a situation, a person needs to hear that forgiveness is divine: God's ways are not our ways (see Isa. 55:8). Part of the good news of forgiveness is that God does not act and feel like us. Other helpful encouragement might include the promise of the Holy Spirit, whose power is beyond ours and whose help is promised to us in the fight against sin (see chapter 6).

- "It happened again. I messed up in the same way I've messed up so many times before. Seems I just can't help it. It's a good thing God is in the forgiveness business!"

  This quote shows a lack of concern for the seriousness and deadliness of sin—as if it is normal for us to be in the "sinning business" and God in the "forgiveness business." In such a situation a person needs to be gently reminded that sin cost God the life of his Son, and that forgiveness is not a right but a gift that we should receive with grateful trust and responsive obedience.

2. In your opinion, which of these is a more common view? Which is most dangerous? Which attitude do you personally tend toward most often?

   While it's strictly a matter of opinion, the second attitude is probably more prevalent in our North American culture. Our society often takes a very light view of sin, preferring to call it a "mistake" or "error in judgment" that God and others should understand and forgive. Within the church, among people who know what sin cost their Savior, perhaps the attitude shown in the first quote is more prevalent. (Group members may offer a third, alternate view as well.) We would regard the second attitude as most dangerous because it fails to acknowledge the seriousness of sin and cheapens a gift that cost God so much.

   On the last part of the question, recognize, of course, that talking about our own attitude toward sin can be intimidating. (What will people think if I say that I'm sometimes inclined to take forgiveness for granted?) You may want to say something that encourages openness and defuses any notion of being judgmental. If participants feel uncomfortable with the two choices given in the question, perhaps you can discuss what we would say if asked about our attitude toward sin and forgiveness in our lives.

DYING WITH A CLEAN SLATE?

Chapter 5 describes an idea that many Christians have about forgiveness: forgiveness is a matter of having all our sins properly identified, confessed, and erased. In this view, it's important that our "slate is clean" before we die. As the chapter suggests, this view has some far-reaching consequences.

1. Do you personally think much or even worry about appearing before God with a "clean slate"? Why or why not?

   You might begin by reading this quote from chapter 5: "We must indeed appear before God with a clean slate. And the fear that we might suddenly have to meet our Judge while there are sins in our lives that have not been confessed and relationships that have not been repaired is terrifying" (p. 67). So this fear or concern is not uncommon or irrational.

2. How does this view turn forgiveness into something earned? What does that do to our assurance and comfort?

It makes forgiveness dependent on confession. While confession is important, it is not the cause of forgiveness. Forgiveness comes from the grace that is ours through the love and sacrifice of Christ. To make forgiveness dependent on anything, even confession, is to take away the assurance and comfort. How could we ever know if our confession was good enough or that we weren't self-deceived?

3. **How might this view actually delay people from living out their full potential as Christians or even put off the decision to be a Christian?**

   Instead of embracing forgiveness and the freedom and energy it brings, this view can degenerate into "bookkeeping." Some people may decide to have some fun first and ask for forgiveness later. It is a mistaken idea about the seriousness of sin and the blessedness of life in God's will.

4. **Why might this view of forgiveness be especially damaging to the spouse of someone suffering from Alzheimer's disease? To the family of someone who committed suicide when they were suffering from depression?**

   Obviously, for persons suffering from dementia or despair, dying "with a clean slate" simply isn't possible. The better view is that such individuals cannot be held accountable for unconfessed sin. All persons, whether in good mental health or not, need to realize we are saved by God's grace, not by our own confessions. "Just trust that your Savior cleans the slate," says chapter 5, "even to the last stains!"

SELF-DISCIPLINE

1. **React to this statement: "You can come to Jesus as you are, but you cannot stay the way you were."**

   You may want to look up a couple of the passages that support this statement (see John 5:14; Matt. 12:45). Participants may want to add examples of individuals who came to Jesus "as they were" but who radically changed after their encounter with Christ.

2. **What comes to mind when you think of "self-discipline" in your own spiritual walk? What helps you discipline yourself so that you grow in holiness?**

   Bible reading/study and prayer are crucial disciplines almost certain to be mentioned. What other means do participants use to grow?

MUTUAL DISCIPLINE (MATTHEW 18:15-20)

Ask someone to read this passage aloud to the group.

1. **Who is Jesus' audience for these instructions? Who is supposed to benefit from the procedure of discipline that Jesus gives?**

   His audience is his disciples. These instructions are given for the benefit of the entire Christian community. The sinner can be forgiven and restored. The community of faith gets to show love, and it keeps itself away from sin.

2. **Review the steps that are involved in trying to correct "a brother [or sister] who sins against you." Why is the order of the steps important? What sort of barriers might prevent the process from being successful?**

   The steps are as follows:

   - *Have a personal meeting with the person in which you talk about how he or she has offended you.*

   - *If the person doesn't listen, take along a couple of witnesses and have a second meeting with the offender.*

   - *If the person still doesn't listen, tell it to the church.*

   - *If the person won't listen to the church, regard that person as no longer a part of the body of Christ but as the object of evangelism.*

   The sequence is important because it asks us to exercise a kind of mutual discipline before we go to the official body, the church. The sequence shows that each member has a personal responsibility in discipline—it's not just the "official" business and responsibility of the church. It's also a gradual process that gives the offending person several opportunities to repent.

   Barriers to the process frequently include a person's being offended at those trying to restore him or her, seeing them as judgmental and self-righteous. Those involved in the process may unknowingly project just such an attitude, forgetting that the whole purpose of the procedure is restoration, not judgment. In addition, individuals and the church itself may be reluctant to initiate the process, fearing that it will only drive the offending person further from repentance and restoration.

3. How does the context of the rest of Matthew 18 help us understand that the whole purpose of discipline is restoration of the sinner?

You may want to refer to the discussion on Matthew 18 "Our Church Manual" (p. 72) as you open your Bibles to that passage. Does the group agree with the interpretation that "little ones" (vv. 6, 10, 14) means "ordinary believers"?

Note especially verse 14, in which God is portrayed as seeking out the lost sheep, unwilling "that any of these little ones should be lost." Notice too how the parable of the unmerciful servant describes "the mercy that must flow from the king, through his servants, to our debtors." In our opinion, all this clearly shows us that the intent of the discipline described in verses 15-20 is restoration of the sinner.

4. What's the significance of Jesus' concluding remark (v. 20) about him being present with his people? What does that have to do with the matter of church discipline?

This is about maintaining the integrity of the body of Christ. He is present with his people. And when we act with integrity and according to his will, Christ is present in those decisions—even the difficult ones outlined in these verses.

CLOSING

Is there a change that you would like to make in your personal walk with God? Perhaps a way to increase your self-discipline? Or a way to be more encouraging and helpful to someone you know? Share your thoughts with the group, if you wish.

Be ready to begin with your own example, if needed. And of course keep this strictly voluntary, acknowledging that there are some things that simply cannot be shared with the entire group.

In your closing prayer, ask the Spirit to fill us and enable us to become more like Jesus. You may want to have a time of silence during which group members may offer their own private prayers for help and guidance.

THE PRACTICE OF FORGIVENESS IN THE CHURCH: SELF-DISCIPLINE AND MUTUAL DISCIPLINE

INTRODUCTION

Stanza 42 of *Our World Belongs to God: A Contemporary Testimony* nicely summarizes what this session is all about. To open today's session, you may want to read it together.

The church is a gathering of forgiven sinners,
called to be holy,
dedicated to service.
Saved by the patient grace of God,
we deal patiently with others.
Knowing our own weakness and failures,
we bring good news to all sinners
with understanding of their condition,
and with hope in God.

FORGIVENESS AND DISCIPLINE

1. How would you respond, or what guidance would you give, to someone in your church or small group Bible study who said:

   • "I keep failing to live like I know I should. I feel like a failure as a Christian. I'm sick and tired of going back to God with the same old sins, asking for forgiveness again and again. And I bet God feels the same way."

   • "It happened again. I messed up in the same way I've messed up so many times before. Seems I just can't help it. It's a good thing God is in the forgiveness business!"

2. In your opinion, which of these is a more common view? Which is most dangerous? Which attitude do you personally tend toward most often?

DYING WITH A CLEAN SLATE?

Chapter 5 describes an idea that many Christians have about forgiveness: that forgiveness is a matter of having all our sins properly identified, confessed, and erased. In this view, it's important that our "slate is clean" before we die. As the chapter suggests, this view has some far-reaching consequences.

1. Do you personally think much or even worry about appearing before God with a "clean slate?" Why or why not?

2. How does this view turn forgiveness into something earned? What does that do to our assurance and comfort?

3. How might this view actually delay people from living out their full potential as Christians or even put off the decision to be a Christian?

4. Why might this view of forgiveness be especially damaging to the spouse of someone suffering from Alzheimer's disease? To the family of someone who committed suicide when they were suffering from depression?

SELF-DISCIPLINE

1. React to this statement: "You can come to Jesus as you are, but you cannot stay the way you were."

2. What comes to mind when you think of "self-discipline" in your own spiritual walk? What helps you discipline yourself so that you grow in holiness?

MUTUAL DISCIPLINE (MATTHEW 18:15-20)

1. Who is Jesus' audience for these instructions? Who is supposed to benefit from the procedure of discipline that Jesus gives?

2. Review the steps that are involved in trying to correct "a brother [or sister] who sins against you." Why is the order of the steps important? What sort of barriers might prevent the process from being successful?

3. How does the context of the rest of Matthew 18 help us understand that the whole purpose of discipline is restoration of the sinner?

4. What's the significance of Jesus' concluding remark (v. 20) about him being present with his people? What does that have to do with the matter of church discipline?

CLOSING

Is there a change that you would like to make in your personal walk with God? Perhaps a way to increase your self-discipline? Or a way to be more encouraging and helpful to someone you know? Share your thoughts with the group, if you wish.

THE PRACTICE OF FORGIVENESS
IN THE CHURCH: OFFICIAL DISCIPLINE

CHAPTER SUMMARY

Last time we saw that self-discipline and mutual discipline are essential practices within the church. In today's session we look at a third way the church practices forgiveness: by official or church discipline.

Church discipline includes the whole teaching/preaching and serving ministry of the church; however, when a member fails to participate in this congregational endeavor, he or she must be encouraged and possibly corrected. Such an act of love is a form of discipline and is the duty of those charged with the pastoral care of the congregation.

Disciplining members today is difficult, due in part to the widespread notion that one needn't be a member of a church to be a Christian. Yet church discipline is clearly biblical and must be applied. The congregation gets its authority to exclude a member from the apostolic authority described in Matthew 18. This action by the church is the third means of dealing with someone who persists in sin—self-discipline and mutual discipline must come first. All church discipline must be aimed at restoration.

In Paul's writings, when a member engages in wrong teaching or bad behavior, the congregation must not treat that person as if everything is normal. He or she should be warned as a brother or sister, and if all other measures fail, be cut off from the fellowship of believers (2 Thess. 3; 1 Cor. 5). However, even in the case of severe offenses, discipline is aimed at restoring the wandering member. And discipline must always be administered with gentleness and an awareness of our own weaknesses.

The unpardonable sin is the deliberate rejection of the Son of God by those who have first tasted the love and power of God's salvation in Christ. The dreadful words about the unpardonable sin were written so that we should cling to the gospel and hold on to each other. What we have received in Christ is life itself.

In forgiveness, the past is not forgotten, but the pain and punishment have been removed. That also means that forgiven sins may have disabled us for certain functions in the present sanctified life. Forgiveness does not undo the past—nothing can—but forgiveness takes the sting out of it so that we can be useful in the present. And the future presents no threat because our Judge is our Savior.

SCRIPTURE REFERENCES

Matthew 18:12-14; Mark 3:29; Romans 8:1, 33-34; Hebrews 6:4-6; 10:26-27

SESSION GOALS

- Describe church discipline as Scripture intends it to be.

- Recognize the necessity of church discipline.

- Describe the unpardonable sin.

- Feel assured that our forgiveness in Christ has taken the sting out of our past, enables us to serve in the present, and allows us to look at the future without fear.

LEADER'S COPY, HANDOUT, SESSION 6
THE PRACTICE OF FORGIVENESS IN THE CHURCH: OFFICIAL DISCIPLINE

INTRODUCTION

Today's session continues the previous chapter's discussion of the practice of forgiveness in the church. In the previous chapter we focused on self-discipline and mutual discipline. Today we look at "official" or church discipline—why it's important and how it should work.

Begin by reading Matthew 18:12-14. Share your thoughts on what this passage suggests to you about church discipline.

The tender picture of a shepherd searching for one lost sheep puts church discipline in exactly the right light—it's not a harsh exclusion of sinners but a loving search to restore the lost one to the fold. You may want to read these words from chapter 6: "If the Spirit of the Good Shepherd lives in the congregation (Matt. 18:12-14), someone is always looking for the wandering. And those charged with pastoral care must look for the straying sheep. It's been our experience that when wanderers return and are forgiven, they often testify that God used the loving persistence of a fellow Christian who kept contact without being judgmental but with the obvious intention of bringing the sinner home" (p. 75).

Option: Alternate Opening

Stanza 42 of Our World Belongs to God *certainly fits this session as well as the previous one. You may want to re-read this section together (see p. 33), either now or at the end of today's session.*

CHURCH DISCIPLINE: IS IT STILL FEASIBLE?

1. Chapter 6 says church discipline "has hardly ever worked as God intended." Do you agree or disagree? Why is disciplining members often so difficult for churches today?

    Please see chapter 6, "Church Discipline: Is It Still Feasible?" (p. 75), for some reasons for the difficulty of church discipline. However, you should also defer to any in your group who have served as elders or deacons and who are therefore familiar with the immediate problems of restoring members who have walked away from the church.

2. How would you respond to this argument: "Look, it's not going to do a lick of good if we elders go and talk to so-and-so. It's far too late to save his marriage anyway. And if we go there and tell him he's wrong in leaving his wife for someone else, it's just going to drive him away from the church. He'll just transfer his membership somewhere else. Times have changed. We have to let these things work themselves out."

    While it's true that often such elder visits seem to do little apparent good, those entrusted with the pastoral care of the congregation must act in such a situation. To do nothing is to neglect what the Bible clearly teaches. And it may suggest to the offender that the church does not care. Such situations obviously demand patience, courage, and a loving, discipling approach.

3. What does the goal of discipline—restoration—suggest about how we go about this task in the church?

    It rules out power plays and judgmental actions of all sorts. It suggests a discipling approach that calls for patience and an acute awareness of our own failures. Only as a last resort should the church sever ties with those who have de-

liberately placed themselves outside of the body. See *stanza 42 of* Our World Belongs to God *for a beautiful statement of all this.*

4. What can we do to help those who seem to have turned their backs on the church?

    Like the Good Shepherd who searches long and hard for his lost sheep, we can be persistent in our prayers for someone we know who needs encouragement or who has lost his or her way. And we can do our best to be encouraging and honest in our contacts with this person. Turning our backs is not the way to lead the lost home.

THE UNPARDONABLE SIN

1. According to Scripture, what is the nature of this sin?

    You may want to look up some of the passages cited in chapter 6: Mark 3:29; Hebrews 6:4-6; 10:26-27. According to the chapter, "The unpardonable sin is the rebellion of the son or daughter who was close to God's heart and who then spit in God's face" (p. 81).

2. Should we worry about falling into this sin? Why or why not?

    Perhaps group members know of persons who, near death, professed great concern about committing this sin. They (and we) ought not to worry about it. You may want to read Romans 8:1, 33-34 as reassurance that God does not condemn those who are in Christ.

3. What can we learn from the biblical descriptions of this sin?

    While we ought not to worry about committing this sin, we do need to recognize how precious our salvation is. You may want to read the last two paragaphs of "The Unpardonable Sin" (pp. 81-82). Perhaps your group can add other ideas as well.

PAST, PRESENT, AND FUTURE

1. Comment on this statement: "Saying that we have been forgiven does not mean that we have no past, just because our sins have been forgiven. Forgiving is not forgetting" (p. 82).

    We cannot forget the sins of the past, nor can the past be undone. In fact, our past sins may disqualify us for doing some things in the present (see p. 83).

2. **Knowing that the past is not forgotten, how should we view it? What about the present and the future?**

Although the past contains sin and brokenness, its sting has been removed, so we can be at peace with it. We have been cleansed and the Father has embraced us in love. Knowing that, we can be useful in the present and live with peace and joy. And we may face the future without fear because the judge is also our Savior.

CLOSING

Pray for your church, giving thanks for its care, remembering its needs, and interceding for its leaders, especially as they are involved in caring for the people of God.

You may also want to invite people to pray—without mentioning names—for persons in the congregation who are in need of spiritual encouragement or who seem to have lost their way.

Option: Alternative Closing

Ask the group to reflect on these statements from the end of chapter 6:

- *"The worst of sinners has been forgiven so that none of us should despair."*

- *"We have received forgiveness, and we extend forgiveness to one another."*

- *"Forgiveness does not undo the past—nothing can—but forgiveness takes the sting out of it so that we can be useful in the present."*

- *"And the future holds no threat because our Judge is our Savior."*

Read the statements aloud to the group, taking your time and speaking with conviction. Then ask for a time of prayer, during which people may express their thanks to God for his instrument of grace, the church, and for his pardon of all our sins.

THE PRACTICE OF FORGIVENESS
IN THE CHURCH: OFFICIAL DISCIPLINE

INTRODUCTION

Today's session continues the previous chapter's discussion of the practice of forgiveness in the church. Last time we focused on self-discipline and mutual discipline. Today we look at "official" or church discipline—why it's important and how it should work.

Begin by reading Matthew 18:12-14. Share your thoughts on what this passage suggests to you about church discipline.

CHURCH DISCIPLINE: IS IT STILL FEASIBLE?

1. Chapter 6 says church discipline "has hardly ever worked as God intended." Do you agree or disagree? Why is disciplining members often so difficult for churches today?

2. How would you respond to this argument: "Look, it's not going to do a lick of good if we elders go and talk to so-and-so. It's far too late to save his marriage anyway. And if we go there and tell him he's wrong in leaving his wife for someone else, it's just going to drive him away from the church. He'll just transfer his membership somewhere else. Times have changed. We have to let these things work themselves out."

3. What does the goal of discipline—restoration—suggest about how we go about this task in the church?

4. What can we do to help those who seem to have turned their backs on the church?

THE UNPARDONABLE SIN

1. According to Scripture, what is the nature of this sin?

2. Should we worry about falling into this sin? Why or why not?

3. What can we learn from the biblical descriptions of this sin?

PAST, PRESENT, AND FUTURE

1. Comment on this statement: "Saying that we have been forgiven does not mean that we have no past, just because our sins have been forgiven. Forgiving is not forgetting" (p. 82).

2. Knowing that the past is not forgotten, how should we view it? What about the present and the future?

CLOSING

Pray for your church, giving thanks for its care, remembering its needs, and interceding for its leaders, especially as they are involved in caring for the people of God.

FORGIVENESS AND RECONCILIATION

CHAPTER SUMMARY

The goal of forgiveness is reconciliation. The deepest purpose behind the incarnation and beyond the cross is that we might be reconciled to our heavenly Father. With the wedge of sin that stood between God and us now removed, we may approach the throne of grace and call God "Abba"—Father.

Many things can lead us to question our identity as God's children. For example, our own consciences may testify that we are unworthy of this honor. But God has the final word on the matter, and he has spoken of his love for us through the gift of Jesus.

Scripture also speaks of the goal of forgiveness in terms of the forgiven being "a new creation." Sin is a corruption of our entire nature. Therefore, for salvation to be effective it takes nothing less than a new nature, so that we not only *do* good but *are* good. We receive the new nature by being "in Christ." Putting on the new nature happens when we die and rise with Christ, or, when we are "born again." This reality of who we are in Christ—forgiven, reconciled and new creatures—is grasped by faith and lived by the Spirit.

Adoption into the family of God is the central, defining characteristic for a Christian. There is no more important quality than whether or not one is "in Christ." So much so that other factors we use to divide and separate people have lost their significance. What binds us together "in Christ" is stronger and of greater importance than anything that might separate us: "There is neither Jew nor Greek, slave nor free, male nor female, for you are all one in Christ Jesus" (Gal. 3:28).

Salvation is not just a destination; it is an entire mode of existence, a way of life. The Spirit is the power that enables the forgiven to "live into" the new reality of who they are in Christ. They must live in a way that shows they are kingdom people and followers of Christ. Only in this setting can the call to forgive one another be properly understood. As part of the new creation reconciled to Christ, we are called to be ambassadors and practitioners of reconciliation. Forgiveness is the tool we are given to restore relationships and heal what has been wounded.

But the road to forgiving and reconciling with others is the same road Jesus walked—carrying a cross. Of all the ways we are called to imitate our Lord, forgiveness and reconciliation are the hardest.

The goal of the cross is nothing less than the renewal of *all* creation. The Creator entered the fallen world, and by his sacrifice, he has decisively turned the course of a rebellious creation back to himself.

SESSION GOALS

- Explore the relationship between forgiveness and reconciliation.

- Describe who we are in and through the work of Christ.

- Discover the interplay between faith and the work of the Spirit in living out our identity as children of God.

- Gain an appreciation for the scope of forgiveness in the past, present, and future.

SCRIPTURE REFERENCES

John 1:12; John 15:15; Romans 5:10-11; Ephesians 2:6, 10; 1 Corinthians 3:16; 1 Peter 2:9-10; 1 John 5:18; Revelation 5:11; Philemon (optional)

**LEADER'S COPY, HANDOUT, SESSION 7
FORGIVENESS AND RECONCILIATION**

INTRODUCTION

This chapter explores reconciliation, the ultimate goal of forgiveness. What sin has separated, God is bringing together to be never separated again.

Which do you find harder to believe: that Jesus died for your sins or that you are a new creation? Why?

There's no right answer here, of course. Both concepts can be extremely hard to believe! That the Son of God chose to die for your sins and mine is an example of love that goes far beyond our human ability to understand. And when we look at our daily struggles with sin, we may not see much convincing evidence of the new life we are supposed to be enjoying in Christ. Both statements, however, are as sure as God's Word to us. They are cornerstones of our faith.

OUR NEW IDENTITY

1. Listed below are a series of statements from Scripture that tell us who we are, in and through the work of Christ.

   In Christ, you are

   - a child of God (John 1:12).

   - God's handiwork, created in Christ to do good works (Eph. 2:10).

   - a member of a royal priesthood, a holy nation, a people for God's own possession (1 Pet. 2:9-10).

   - born of God and out of the reach of the evil one (1 John 5:18).

   - a dwelling place for his Holy Spirit (1 Cor. 3:16).

   - the friend of Christ (John 15:15).

   - a citizen of heaven, seated with Christ in the heavenly places (Eph. 2:6).

   When you hear these descriptions from God's Word, what emotions do they evoke? Which takes the most faith to believe?

   Look back through the list once more. In what ways are these descriptions both *gifts* and *tasks*?

   Have group members take turns reading the statements and the supporting Scripture. Take your time, pausing between each statement for a moment of reflection. Ask participants to tell how these statements make them feel. Secure? Joyful? Grateful? Amazed? Doubtful? Something else? Do any of the statements stand out as more difficult to believe than others?

   We are all of these things through the work of Christ, and through his love he bestows them as gifts to us. But they also become our task—we must live into our new identity. Our conduct should show us to be like our Father. We are created by Christ to do good works; we are expected to produce fruit; as part of a royal priesthood we are called to holiness, and so on.

2. Do you agree or disagree with this statement: "We have too often reduced the gospel to the question of personal salvation, just Jesus and me . . ." (p. 93)?

   The danger is that we fail to realize that the gospel changes everything! It "transforms how we see ourselves, how we see each other, and how we see this world." We fail to recognize that the gospel "restores a fragmented humanity into the single family of God." We forget that "the goal of forgiveness is reconciliation."

Option: Remarkable Reconciliation, A.D. 60

If time permits, you may want to talk about the story of Onesimus as an example of reconciliation (see p. 93). Read this short book (25 verses); then talk about questions like these:

- *How had Onesimus "offended" Philemon? (v. 18). According to the social pattern of the day, what "rights" did Philemon have over his runaway slave?*

- *On what basis does Paul tell Philemon to regard Onesimus as a brother, not as a slave? What changed everything?*

- *What do you think might be a similar example of "reconciliation in Christ" today?*

LIVING OUT OUR NEW IDENTITY—
THE POWER OF THE SPIRIT

1. Being saved is not only a matter of being joined to the person of Christ, but joined to the program of Christ. And we must be consistent in living according to our faith. "'To claim the comfort of the Crucified while rejecting his way is to advocate not only cheap grace but a deceitful ideology'" (p. 95).

   Why is it tempting to want just the person of Christ but not his program? What is his program? To what kind of tasks does it call us?

   The program of Christ calls us to become new creations. It means battling the power of sin, working for redemption, taking up our cross, and following him. This is hard work, and we are reluctant to go through the pain it will entail. Forgiveness is one of the critical tasks in this program.

2. "Forgiveness is the tool we are given to restore relationships and heal what has been wounded. The continual temptation is to use the tools that our broken world employs . . . to fight bad temper with

bad temper, bitterness with bitterness, injury by injuring" (p. 95).

Give some examples, both major and minor, of using "the tools that our broken world employs" when we've been hurt. Why are we so often tempted to react in these ways?

Examples may range from tailgating a motorist who has cut us off in a fit of road rage to remaining openly hostile to a spouse who has divorced us. You may want to talk about how even within the church we sometimes harbor grudges against fellow believers who have offended us in some way.

As chapter 7 points out, we are tempted to react in these ways because "we are the victim, we are the injured party." But retaliation is the method of the evil one. The power of Christ works through the power of love, which redeems and transforms. It often appears more like powerlessness than like any sort of strength, and so we are reluctant to use it.

3. Suppose that a member of your family has been run down and killed by a drunken driver, someone who had a long record of driving while intoxicated. What might forgiveness and reconciliation look like in such a circumstance? Are both necessary?

You may want to read the quote from Miroslav Volf that points out forgiveness and reconciliation are distinct, and that reconciliation may sometimes be out of reach (p. 96). Yet, he says, Christ's passion is aimed at peace, at communion between former enemies. Note also Ron Feenstra's comments (in endnote 5) about the limits of reconciliation.

After your discussion, you may want to reflect on our own reconciliation to God, as described in Romans 5:10-11: "For if, when we were God's enemies, we were reconciled to him through the death of his Son, how much more, having been reconciled, shall we be saved through his life! Not only is this so, but we also rejoice in God through our Lord Jesus Christ, through whom we have now received reconciliation."

4. "The Spirit is the power that enables us to live the new life in Christ" (p. 95). In your own experience, have you felt the need for the power of the Spirit to help you live the new life? In what ways does the Spirit help you do that?

The Spirit testifies to our spirits that we are God's children, the Spirit empowers us to obey, the Spirit gives us peace.

THE COSMIC GOAL OF FORGIVENESS

1. "We tend to think of forgiveness in personal terms." Is this true of you? Comment.

Be sure to affirm the validity of thinking of forgiveness in this way. If it's not personal, it's not real!

2. How can it help our faith to know that forgiveness extends to the whole creation, that the fallen world itself will be renewed by the sacrifice of Christ?

It's a sign of how powerful and loving and awesome God is—not just toward us, but to the world itself! This speaks of God's love for the world and of Christ's complete victory over sin and evil. No power in heaven or on earth will be able to separate us from the love of God in Christ!

3. In your own words, how does God's forgiveness and reconciliation affect your past? Your present? Your future?

Group members may want to refer to the last few paragraphs of chapter 7, but invite them to say for themselves what God's forgiveness means to them in the past, the present, and the future.

CLOSING

Say together the song of the redeemed in heaven (Rev. 5:12):

"Worthy is the lamb who was slain
to receive power and wealth and wisdom and strength
and honor and glory and praise!"

If you have time, ask someone to read the context of this song (Rev. 5:9-11, 13-14). Have the group say verse 12 (above) in unison.

Option: Alternate Closing

Instead of the above, remind the group of the picture of the forgiving father embracing the prodigal son: "But while he was still a long way off, his father saw him and was filled with compassion for him; he ran to his son, threw his arms around him and kissed him" (Luke 15:20).

You may also want to read this from the opening page of chapter 7:

> We are forgiven, so we have a restored Father-child relationship with our Lord. Reconciled to one another through the cross of Christ, we now see each other as brothers and sisters. . . The Bible does not talk of forgiveness in the abstract. In fact, forgiveness triumphs precisely because it is so personal. I discover that God's forgiveness has my name on it. And the forgiving Father looks down the road, waiting to run and embrace me and restore me to his family.
>
> The eternal, all-encompassing rationale for forgiveness is reconciliation. With the wedge of sin that stood between God and us now removed, we may approach the throne of grace, [saying], "Our Father . . . in heaven."

Invite the group to pray whatever is on their hearts, beginning their prayers with the words that describe our new relationship to God: "Our Father . . ."

FORGIVENESS AND RECONCILIATION

INTRODUCTION

This chapter explores reconciliation, the ultimate goal of forgiveness. What sin has separated, God is bringing together to be never separated again.

Which do you find harder to believe: that Jesus died for your sins or that you are a new creation? Why?

OUR NEW IDENTITY

1. Listed below are a series of statements from Scripture that tell us who we are, in and through the work of Christ.

In Christ, you are

- a child of God (John 1:12).

- God's handiwork, created in Christ to do good works (Eph. 2:10).

- a member of a royal priesthood, a holy nation, a people for God's own possession (1 Pet. 2:9-10).

- born of God and out of the reach of the evil one (1 John 5:18).

- a dwelling place for his Holy Spirit (1 Cor. 3:16).

- the friend of Christ (John 15:15).

- a citizen of heaven, seated with Christ in the heavenly places (Eph. 2:6).

When you hear these descriptions from God's Word, what emotions do they evoke? Which takes the most faith to believe?

Look back through the list once more. In what ways are these descriptions both *gifts* and *tasks*?

2. Do you agree or disagree with this statement: "We have too often reduced the gospel to the question of personal salvation, just Jesus and me . . ." (p. 93)? What's the danger of this view?

LIVING OUT OUR NEW IDENTITY— THE POWER OF THE SPIRIT

1. Being saved is not only a matter of being joined to the person of Christ, but joined to the program of Christ. And we must be consistent in living according to our faith. "'To claim the comfort of the Crucified while rejecting his way is to advocate not only cheap grace but a deceitful ideology'" (p. 95).

Why is it tempting to want just the person of Christ but not his program? What is his program? To what kind of tasks does it call us?

2. "Forgiveness is the tool we are given to restore relationships and heal what has been wounded. The continual temptation is to use the tools that our broken world employs . . . to fight bad temper with bad temper, bitterness with bitterness, injury by injuring" (p. 95).

Give some examples, both major and minor, of using "the tools that our broken world employs" when we've been hurt. Why are we so often tempted to react in these ways?

3. Suppose that a member of your family has been run down and killed by a drunken driver, someone who had a long record of driving while intoxicated. What might forgiveness and reconciliation look like in such a circumstance? Are both necessary?

4. "The Spirit is the power that enables us to live the new life in Christ" (p. 95). In your own experience, have you felt the need for the power of the Spirit to help you live the new life? In what ways does the Spirit help you do that?

THE COSMIC GOAL OF FORGIVENESS

1. "We tend to think of forgiveness in personal terms." Is this true of you? Comment.

2. How can it help our faith to know that forgiveness extends to the whole creation, that the fallen world itself will be renewed by the sacrifice of Christ?

3. In your own words, how does God's forgiveness and reconciliation affect your past? Your present? Your future?

CLOSING

Say together the song of the redeemed in heaven (Rev. 5:12):

"Worthy is the lamb who was slain
to receive power and wealth and wisdom and strength
and honor and glory and praise!"